# Starting with... Role play

## Emergency 999

Diana Bentley
Maggie Hutchings
Dee Reid

Diana Bentley is an educational consultant for primary literacy and has written extensively for both teachers and children. She worked for many years in the Centre for the Teaching of Reading at Reading University and then became a Senior Lecturer in Primary English at Oxford Brookes University. Throughout her professional life she has continued to work in schools and teach children aged from 5 to 11 years.

Maggie Hutchings has considerable experience teaching KS1 and Early Years. She is a Leading Teacher for literacy in The Foundation Stage and is a Foundation Stage and Art coordinator. Maggie is passionate about the importance of learning through play and that learning should be an exciting and fun experience for young children. Her school's art work has been exhibited in The National Gallery, London.

Dee Reid is a former teacher who has been an independent consultant in primary literacy for over 20 years in many local authorities. She is consultant to 'Catch Up' – a special needs literacy intervention programme used in over 4,000 schools in the UK. She is Series Consultant to 'Storyworlds' (Heinemann) and her recent publications include 'Think About It' (Nelson Thornes) and Literacy World (Heinemann).

Other titles in the series:

Colour and light
Under the ground
Into space
At the hospital
Fairytales
At the garage/At the airport
All creatures great and small
On the farm
Water
Ourselves
At the shops

Other Foundation titles:

Starting with stories and poems:

Self esteem
Self care
A sense of community
Making relationships
Behaviour and self control

A collection of stories and poems

Starting with our bodies and movement

Starting with sounds and letters

---

The authors would like to thank Jane Whitwell for all her hard work in compiling the resources and poems for the series.

---

Published by
Hopscotch Educational Publishing Ltd, Unit 2, The Old Brushworks, 56 Pickwick Road, Corsham, Wiltshire, SN13 9BX
Tel: 01249 701701

© 2006 Hopscotch Educational Publishing

Written by Diana Bentley, Maggie Hutchings and Dee Reid
Series design by Blade Communications
Cover illustration by Sami Sweeten
Illustrated by Debbie Clark
Printed by Colorman (Ireland) Ltd

ISBN 1 905390 15 7

Diana Bentley, Maggie Hutchings and Dee Reid hereby assert their moral right to be identified as the authors of this work in accordance with the Copyright, Designs and Patents Act, 1988.

The authors and publisher would like to thank Chapter One (a specialist children's bookshop) in Wokingham for all their help and support. Email: chapteronebookshop@yahoo.co.uk

All rights reserved. This book is sold subject to the condition that it shall not, by way of trade or otherwise, be lent, hired out or otherwise circulated without the publisher's prior consent in any form of binding or cover other than that in which it is published and without a similar condition, including this condition, being imposed upon the subsequent purchaser.

No part of this publication may be reproduced, stored in a retrieval system, or transmitted, in any form or by any means, electronic, mechanical, photocopying, recording or otherwise, without the prior permission of the publisher, except where photocopying for educational purposes within the school or other educational establishment that has purchased this book is expressly permitted in the text.

**Starting** with role play – Emergency 999

# Contents

| | |
|---|---|
| Introduction | 4 |
| 'Emergency 999' planning chart | 6 |
| Week 1 – Creating the police station | 7 |
| Week 2 – Making poster and ID cards | 11 |
| Week 3 – Creating a fire station | 16 |
| Week 4 – Safety in the home | 20 |
| Week 5 – Creating an ambulance | 24 |
| Week 6 – People who help us | 28 |
| Photocopiables | 32 |

## Acknowledgements

The authors and publisher gratefully acknowledge permission to reproduce copyright material in this book.

'The Local Fire Brigade' from *The Bee's Knees* by Roger McGough (copyright © Roger McGough, 2003) is reproduced by permission of PFD (www.pfd.co.uk) on behalf of Roger McGough.

Every effort has been made to trace the owners of copyright of material in this book and the publisher apologises for any inadvertent omissions. Any persons claiming copyright for any material should contact the publisher who will be happy to pay the permission fees agreed between them and who will amend the information in this book on any subsequent reprint.

# Introduction

There are 12 books in the series **Starting with role play** offering a complete curriculum for the Early Years.

Ourselves                 At the garage/At the airport
Into space                Emergency 999
At the shops              All creatures great and small
Colour and light          Under the ground
At the hospital           Fairytales
On the farm               Water

While each topic is presented as a six-week unit of work, it can easily be adapted to run for fewer weeks if necessary. The themes have been carefully selected to appeal to boys and girls and to a range of cultural groups.

Each unit addresses all six areas of learning outlined in the *Curriculum Guidance for the Foundation Stage* and the specific Early Learning Goal is identified for each activity and indicated by this symbol.

Generally, differentiation is achieved by outcome, although for some of the Communication, Language and Literacy strands and Mathematical Development strands, extension activities are suggested for older or more confident learners.

### Suggested teaching sequence for each unit

Each week has been organised into a suggested teaching sequence. However, each activity in an area of learning links to other activities and there will be overlap as groups engage with the tasks.

### The Core Curriculum: Literacy and Mathematics

Every school will have its own programmes for literacy and mathematics and it is not intended that the activities in the units in this book should replace these. Rather, the activities suggested aim to support any programme, to help to consolidate the learning and to demonstrate how the learning can be used in practical situations.

## The importance of role play

'Children try out their most recent learning, skills and competences when they play. They seem to celebrate what they know.'

Tina Bruce (2001) *Learning Through Play: Babies, Toddlers and the Foundation Years.* London: Hodder & Stoughton.

Early Years practitioners are aware of the importance of play as a vehicle for learning. When this play is carefully structured and managed then the learning opportunities are greatly increased. Adult participation can be the catalyst for children's imaginations and creativity.

Six weeks allows for a role play area to be created, developed and expanded and is the optimum time for inspiring children and holding their interest. It is important not to be too prescriptive in the role play area. Teachers should allow for children's ideas and interests to evolve and allow time for the children to explore and absorb information. Sometimes, the children will take the topic off at a tangent or go into much greater depth than expected or even imagined.

### Organising the classroom

The role play area could be created by partitioning off a corner of the classroom with ceiling drapes, an old-style clothes-horse, chairs, boxes, large-scale construction blocks (for example, 'Quadro') or even an open-fronted beach tent/shelter. Alternatively, the whole classroom could be dedicated to the role play theme.

### Involving parents and carers

Encourage the children to talk about the topic and what they are learning with their parents or carers at home. With adult help and supervision, they can explore the internet and search for pictures in magazines and books. This enriches the learning taking place in the classroom.

### Outside activities

The outdoor classroom should be an extension of the indoor classroom and it should support and enhance the activities offered inside. Boys, in particular, often feel less restricted in outdoor play. They may use language more purposefully and may even engage more willingly in reading and writing activities. In the

# Introduction

outdoor area things can be done on a much bigger, bolder and noisier scale and this may connect with boys' preferred learning styles.

Observation in Salford schools and settings noted that boys access books much more readily when there is a book area outdoors.

## Resources

Role play areas can be more convincing reconstructions when they are stocked with authentic items. Car boot sales, jumble sales and charity shops are good sources of artefacts. It is a good idea to inform parents and carers of topics well in advance so they can be looking out for objects and materials that will enhance the role play area.

## Reading

Every week there should be a range of opportunities for children to participate in reading experiences. These should include:

*Shared reading*

The practitioner should read aloud to the children from Big Books, modelling the reading process; for example, demonstrating that print is read from left to right. Shared reading also enables the practitioner to draw attention to high frequency words, the spelling patterns of different words and punctuation. Where appropriate, the practitioner should cover words and ask the children to guess which word would make sense in the context. This could also link with phonic work where the children could predict the word based on seeing the initial phoneme. Multiple readings of the same text enable them to become familiar with story language and tune in to the way written language is organised into sentences.

*Independent reading*

As children become more confident with the written word they should be encouraged to recognise high frequency words. Practitioners should draw attention to these words during shared reading and shared writing. Children should have the opportunity to read these words in context and to play word matching and word recognition games. Encourage the children to use their ability to hear the sounds at various points in words and to use their knowledge of those phonemes to decode simple words.

## Writing

*Shared writing*

Writing opportunities should include teacher demonstration, teacher scribing, copy writing and independent writing. (Suggestions for incorporating shared writing are given each week.)

*Emergent writing*

The role play area should provide ample opportunities for children to write purposefully, linking their writing with the task in hand. These meaningful writing opportunities help children to understand more about the writing process and to seek to communicate in writing. Children's emergent writing should occur alongside their increasing awareness of the 'correct' form of spellings. In the example below, the child is beginning to have an understanding of letter shapes as well as the need to write from left to right.

## Assessment

When children are actively engaged in the role play area this offers ample opportunities for practitioners to undertake observational assessments. By participating in the role play area the practitioner can take time to talk in role to the children about their work and assess their performance. The assessment grid on page 44 enables practitioners to record progress through the appropriate Stepping Stone or Early Learning Goal.

## DfES publications

The following publications will be useful:

*Progression in Phonics* (DfES 0178/2000)
*Developing Early Writing* (DfES 0055/2001)
*Playing with Sounds* (DfES 0280/2004)

# 'Emergency 999' planning chart

| Emergency 999 | Role play area | Personal, Social and Emotional Development | Communication, Language and Literacy | Knowledge and Understanding of the World | Mathematical Development | Creative Development | Physical Development |
|---|---|---|---|---|---|---|---|
| Week 1 | Creating the police station | *Continue to be interested, excited and motivated to learn* <br> Talking about the police and their role in the community | *Listen with enjoyment and respond to songs and rhymes* <br> Making a sign for the police station <br> Making labels for the police station | *Find out about past and present* <br> Learning about the work of the police today and in the past | *Use language such as 'taller', 'shorter' to compare height* <br> Comparing own heights and building taller towers | *Explore colour, texture, shape, form and space* <br> Building the police station and making life-size models of police officers | *Move with control and coordination* <br> Copying movements such as policemen might make |
| Week 2 | Making 'Wanted' posters and ID cards | *Understand what is right and what is wrong and why* <br> Using story as a basis for discussion on right and wrong <br> Talking about being lost | *Speak clearly and audibly with confidence and control* <br> Playing a listening game <br> Making identity cards | *Find out about everyday technology* <br> Making fingerprints and footprints <br> Using cameras to take class photographs | *Use developing mathematical ideas to solve practical problems* <br> Playing the memory game <br> Making a telephone directory | *Use their imagination in art and design* <br> Using a camera to make a 'Wanted' poster and a fingerprint poster | *Travel around, under, over and through* <br> Moving over and through apparatus <br> Being police officers directing the traffic |
| Week 3 | Creating the fire station and the firefighters' pole | *Initiate ideas and speak in a familiar group* <br> Talking about the role of the firefighter | *Enjoy listening to and using spoken and written language* <br> Writing a story about Firefighter Jo | *Ask questions about why things happen and how things work* <br> Roleplaying responding to a 999 emergency | *Use developing mathematical ideas to solve practical problems* <br> Measuring different lengths of hosing | *Explore colour, texture, space and form* <br> Making model fire engines and a firefighters' pole <br> Making a collage of firefighting | *Move with confidence, imagination and in safety* <br> Dancing to music <br> Aiming water pistols accurately |
| Week 4 | Creating a safety poster | *Continue to be interested, excited and motivated to learn* <br> Discussing the dangers of fire | *Attempt writing for different purposes* <br> Creating fire safety posters | *Ask questions about how things happen and why things work* <br> Learning about dangers in the kitchen <br> Discussing the story of the Great Fire of London | *Say and use number names in order* <br> Counting rungs on a ladder <br> Building towers of different heights | *Use their imagination in art* <br> Make various shades of orange <br> Create charcoal drawings | *Move with control and coordination* <br> Playing the firefighters game |
| Week 5 | Creating the interior of an ambulance | *Continue to be interested, excited and motivated to learn* <br> Talking about accidents and how to avoid them | *Use language to imagine and recreate roles* <br> Completing a recount of a paramedic's day <br> Role playing responding to a 999 call | *Find out about and identify objects and events they observe* <br> Using non-fiction books to learn about the ambulance service | *Use developing mathematical ideas to solve practical problems* <br> Programming Roamer to move forwards and backwards <br> Estimating lengths of different bandages | *Explore colour, texture, shape and form* <br> Designing the inside of an ambulance <br> Making a stretcher for a doll | *Move with control and coordination* <br> Making soft dough models <br> Recreating a scene in which a doll is involved in an accident |
| Week 6 | Using the resources of all three emergency services to enhance role play <br> Having a party to celebrate their work | *Work as part of a group, taking turns and sharing fairly* <br> Learning about people in the community who help us | *Read a range of familiar and common words* <br> Writing simple sentences <br> Making invitations for the end of unit party | *Find out about their environment* <br> Role playing responding to an emergency call <br> Discovering simple mapwork and learning about left and right | *Recognise numbers 1–9* <br> Playing the emergency race game <br> Counting objects in hoops | *Use their imagination in art and design* <br> Making party food | *Move with control and coordination* <br> Playing party games including 'Bandage the doll' |

**Starting** with role play – Emergency 999

# Emergency 999

In this six-week unit, the children will investigate and find out about the police, firefighters and the ambulance service. They will concentrate first on the work of the police and create a role play area based on a police station. After two weeks, the police station will be converted into a fire Station. In the final two weeks, the children will become an ambulance crew. If possible, invite personnel from any of the emergency services to visit the class. (You will need to be sensitive to the children's family situations when doing activities related to the police.)

The unit will round off with a party to celebrate the work of people who help us. The children will make food for the party and play party games. At the end of the unit they will have learned about how the main emergency services help us. They will have made:

- a police station
- life-size models of police constables
- portrait photographs, using a digital camera
- identity cards
- junk models of fire engines
- life-size models of firefighters
- fire safety posters
- the interior of an ambulance
- stretchers.

## WEEK 1

### Starting the role play area

During the week the children will create the police station and begin to learn about the role of the police and how they help us from day to day. They will make a **backdrop** for the police station, life-size models of police officers, a **blue light** to hang outside the police station and **signs** such as Police, Enquiry Desk and Interview room. Adults should take on roles such as a police officer and a traffic warden, modelling language appropriate to the role.

**Starting** with role play – Emergency 999

# Creating the police station

## Resources

**Photocopiables:**

Instructions for making the role play backdrop (page 32)
Templates for police officers (page 33)
Poems and songs 1 (page 34)
Police equipment (page 35)

Fiction books:

*Mog, the Forgetful Cat* by Judith Kerr, Collins (0 006640 62 1)
*P.C. Polly* by Mandy Ross, Ladybird (0 721421 68 7)
*Being Lost – A Present for Paul* by Bernard Ashley, Collins (0 006641 60 1)

Non-fiction books:

*People Who Help Us: The Police Force* by Jillian Powell, Wayland (0 750222 52 2)
*A Day in the Life of a Policeman*, Franklin Watts (0 749641 00 2)

Website:

www.bbc.co.uk/cbeebies/balamory/plum/index.shtml

Music and songs:

'The Laughing Policeman': CD: 'Hello Children Everywhere', EMI Gold ASIN B0000647H3

Materials:

- Range of paper, pads, notebooks
- Clipboards
- Large lined book to record events and incidents (incident book)
- Large sheets of frieze paper or backing paper
- Posters about the police
- Leaflets, if possible, from a police station
- Unifix and wooden bricks

Costumes and props:

- Police hats and helmets (for men and women)
- Tabards: could make own simple tabards out of blue fabric 'decorated' using fabric crayons
- Toy police equipment such as: handcuffs, badges, notebooks, whistles, truncheons, radios, walkie-talkies, mobile phones
- Blue lights

NOTE - Be aware that references to the police, cells, fingerprints and so on may distress some children, so omit references as necessary.

## Personal, Social and Emotional Development

*Be interested, excited and motivated to learn.*

### Circle time

- Tell the children that they are going to think about people who help us. Ask them to tell you who they think these people might be. What do these people do? How do they help us?
- Tell the children that they are going to learn about the work of the police and that they are going to create and play in their own police station in the role play area. (Have available some non-fiction books about the police.)
- Begin by talking about the police and their role in the community. For example, the police are our friends; they protect us; they can help lost children find their mums or dads; they help people who need directions; they can help us to cross the road safely; they direct traffic; they control crowds and they try to solve crimes. Emphasise and discuss with the children the positive role of the police: most police stations are open night and day, police officers work in shifts and they deal with emergencies, such as road traffic accidents. Explain that they need to be able to travel to incidents quickly (blue lights and sirens on vehicles).

## Knowledge and Understanding of the World

*Find out about past and present. Find out about people they know.*

### Extending vocabulary

- Together look at posters and pictures of the police. Ask the children why they think the police wear uniforms. Help them to identify some of the other branches of the police force; for example: community police officers, motorway patrols, motorcyclists, helicopter patrols, mounted police, underwater teams, detectives and dog handlers. Ask them if all police officers wear uniforms. Help them to use appropriate vocabulary.

# Creating the police station

- Discuss why a police officer wears a helmet. What is the police officer's 'beat'? What does 'patrol' mean?
- Talk about women in the police force. What does a woman police officer's uniform look like? What does her hat look like?

## Developing the role play area

- Encourage the children to consider how the police station should be created. Where could it be located in the classroom? What will we need to put in it? Is our police station in a village, a town or a city?

### Extension

- Support the children as they find out about the history of the police force (its origin and changes to the uniforms) using information books and the internet. Encourage them to talk about their findings.

### Creative Development

*Explore colour, texture, shape, form and space in two or three dimensions.*

## Building the role play area

- Begin to create the police station (see page 32). Mount the finished scene on the wall of the role play area.

## Making life-size models

- Ask the children to draw round a boy and a girl and cut out the figures. Paint these blue and dress them with collage materials, such as shiny buttons, a police officer's belt, collar numbers and a pair of handcuffs. Display these in the police station and add name labels, such as PC Mackenzie and WPC Jones.

## Blue light

- Make a blue light to hang outside the police station (see page 32).

### Communication, Language and Literacy

*Listen with enjoyment and respond to songs and rhymes. Explore and experiment with sounds, words and texts.*

## Listening and talking

- Share a non-fiction book with the children (see Resources). Discuss the information and encourage the children to use new vocabulary accurately.

## Poems and verse

- Read simple poems about the police, such as 'I'm a tall policeman' (see page 34). These poems and rhymes can be repeated during the first two weeks of the unit.

### Extension

- More able children could learn a poem by heart.

## Making a sign

- Make a sign for the police station. Draw round letter stencils: POLICE. Use a white pencil on a blue background. Ask the children to decorate each letter, making patterns with white pencils. Explain that capital letters are often used for signs. Ask them to look for other signs with capital letters.

## Writing (Teacher scribing)

- Make labels for the police station. Discuss with the children what labels might be needed. Look at information books to get ideas. Scribe the children's suggestions: Enquiry desk, Control room, Cells, Interview room. Ask some children to copy these onto card or write the labels in block lettering and let them colour within the letter shapes.
- Collect pictures of items associated with the police (a whistle, helmet, handcuffs, truncheon, radio or walkie-talkie – see page 35). Sticky tack each item to a class whiteboard and ask the children to help

# Creating the police station

you write labels for them on folded cards and place them alongside the real items. Make duplicate labels and give these to the children to find and match.

**Extension**

❑ Give more able children copies of page 35 and ask them to write labels for each item.

> ## Mathematical Development
> *elg* Use language such as 'taller'/'shorter' to compare height.

### Measuring height

❑ Make several copies of the police officers on page 33. Enlarge them so that you have officers of different heights. Colour them, cut them out and laminate them. Ask the children to put them in order of height, starting with the shortest.

❑ Compare groups of children in the class by height and ask others to put them in order of height. Ask: Who is the tallest? Who is the shortest? Who is taller than Joe? Who is shorter than Emma? Stand a child on a stool or chair and ask: Is he or she taller than Abbie now? Talk about the difference between taller and higher, shorter and lower.

❑ Build a tower of five bricks or blocks and ask the children to build a taller tower. Ask: How many bricks are there in my tower? How many Unifix are there in your tower? Compare the different towers. Repeat this activity, starting with a different number of blocks. The children should eventually be able to play this game independently of an adult.

❑ Have available a one minute sand timer and some wooden bricks. Ask groups of children to see who can build the tallest tower in one minute. Count the bricks.

### Counting rhymes

❑ Recite a counting rhyme (see page 34). Children could 'act out' the rhymes.

> ## Physical Development
> *elg* Move with control and coordination.

### Movement

❑ Say 'Walk like a police officer, standing tall and straight, using slow steps. Stop and hold your shape.' (Use this instruction throughout the activities.) 'Now, march, looking around and changing direction. Next, walk in pairs, trying to match your partner's steps. Now, change direction and use all the spaces. Increase the pace. Walk quickly, looking all around you as you move. In pairs, try to match your partner's steps. Run and change direction, using all the spaces. Don't forget to look before you change direction!'

❑ Ask the children to think of other ways a police officer might move – for example, turning and looking around, looking high and looking low, moving under something low, climbing over something high or squeezing through a narrow space. Encourage the children to practise these movements on their own and then demonstrate to others. Tell the children to work in pairs; one child moves in different ways and his or her partner tries to copy.

**Extension**

❑ A development of this activity could be to make up a sequence of movements together, practise it and perform it to others.

**Starting** with role play – Emergency 999

# Emergency 999

## WEEK 2

### The role play area

During this week, the role play area will be used by the children to investigate similarities and differences in people. They will learn how to use a digital camera to take portrait photographs. They will make individual **ID cards** and be able to say their address and telephone number. They will create **'Wanted' posters** for display in the police station, a **speed camera** and **lost and found cards**.

### Resources

Photocopiables:

Instructions – traffic lights and speed cameras (page 32)
Poems and songs 1 (page 34)
Identity card and outline pictures of cars (page 36)

Fiction books:

*Burglar Bill* by J & A Ahlberg, Puffin (0 140503 01 3)
*Cops and Robbers* by J & A Ahlberg, Puffin (0 140565 84 1)

Non fiction books:

*People Who Help Us: The Police*, Watts (0 749646 68 3)
*Who help us …in the street*, 'Little Nippers' series, Heinemann Library (0 431173 22 2)
*Stay safe … on the road*, 'Little Nippers' series, Heinemann Library (0 431172 71 4)

Materials:

- A selection of pictures of people, faces, boys, girls, men, women, young, old and people of different ethnic origins
- A large piece of fabric to make a screen
- Small notebooks
- Tape recorder
- Digital camera
- Wool (hair colours)
- Fabric scraps
- Decorative beads
- A tray
- Items in the police station
- Black sugar paper
- Talcum powder

Website:

www.bbc.co.uk/cbeebies

Starting with role play – Emergency 999

# Making posters and ID cards

### Personal, Social and Emotional Development

*Understand what is right and what is wrong, and why. Consider the consequences of their words and actions for themselves and others.*

### Listening and discussion

- Read a story about a burglar (see Resources). Give the children time to discuss the story. Is it right or wrong to take other people's things? What else should we not do? Why? What is a crime? Ask the children to give their ideas.

- Give the children a scenario and ask them to decide what is right and what is wrong. For example, describe a situation where a girl is very cross with her mum and when her mum is not looking she deliberately breaks an old cup that is kept at the back of the cupboard. Compare this with a girl who decides to make a cup of tea for her mum. She puts her mum's favourite cup on the tray but she knocks the tray over and the cup is smashed. Which girl does wrong? Discuss the implications.

### Circle time

- Ask the children if they have ever been lost. When? Ask them to describe how they felt: What did you do? Why do you think you got lost? Was the shop very busy? How do you think your mum or dad felt when they realised you were not with them? Who should you go up to? Who could help you?

### Creative Development

*Use their imagination in art and design.*

### Taking photographs

- Show the children how to use a digital camera and, under supervision, let them take photographs of each other. You should obtain permission from parents and carers first. (If you do not have access to a digital camera, use a 35mm or a Polaroid camera.) If possible, show them how the photographs are printed out (thumbnail size). Make two copies. Cut out and laminate one set for the identity parade game (see Knowledge and Understanding of the World). The other set will be used for ID cards.

### Group photos

- Together take group photographs with about eight of them in a line. Ensure that every child has been included. Print these as large as possible, laminate them and use them for the identity parade games.

### 'Wanted' posters

- Give each child a sheet of paper, preferably A4 size, colouring pencils, paints and a selection of collage materials, such as wool (hair colours), fabric scraps and beads. Draw lines at the top and bottom of the paper. Remind the children how everyone looks different. Tell them that they are going to make 'Wanted' posters. Talk about the purpose of the posters. Ask them to close their eyes and make a picture of a person in their minds. Ask: Is your person young or old, a boy or a girl, a man or a woman? What colour hair/eyes has your person? Does he or she have long or short, straight or curly hair? What colour skin does he or she have? Is he or she wearing jewellery? Tell the children they are going to make a portrait of this person. When the portraits have been completed, ask the children to think of a name for their person. Add this name at the bottom. Write: 'Wanted' at the top. The writing could be done by either the children copying from a card or the teacher. Display these posters in or around the police station.

Starting with role play – Emergency 999

# Making posters and ID cards

## Making a fingerprint poster

- Divide a large sheet of paper into squares, one square for each member of the class, including adults. Make an ink pad – a paint-soaked sponge in a tray (or use a commercially produced washable ink pad). Ask each child to make a fingerprint in a square and write his or her name underneath. Using a magnifying glass, compare the fingerprints on the chart. Ask the children if they can detect slight differences between the fingerprints.
- Make a speed camera (see page 32).

### Mathematical Development

*Use developing mathematical ideas and methods to solve practical problems.*

## Memory games

- Play 'Kim's Game' (ideally in the police station). You will need: a tray, a cloth or piece of fabric and items used by a police officer, such as handcuffs, a pencil, a notebook, a badge, a radio and a whistle. Place the objects on the tray. As you do so, name each item. Ask the children to look closely as you are going to take one of the objects away. Cover the tray and remove an object. Uncover the tray and ask, 'What is missing?' Vary the number of objects on the tray according to the ability of the group. Sometimes remove more than one object.
- Talk about the emergency number 999 and how it should only be used in a real emergency. Practise writing 9s in finger paints, in sand (dry and wet) and with chalk in the playground. Make some 9s with dry pasta.

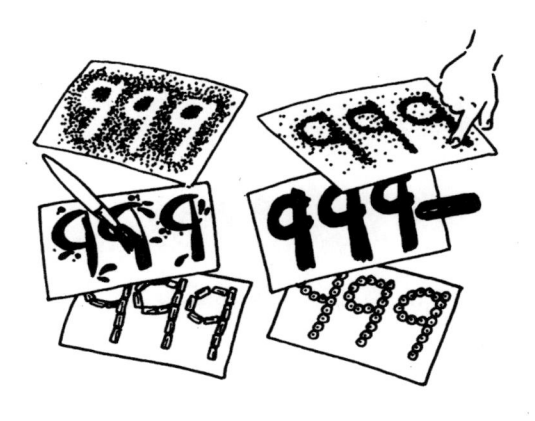

### Extension

- Help the children to create a simple telephone directory for the police station. With the children, make a list of useful numbers. Ask them to draw simple pictures, such as a hospital or a fire station. Add fictitious numbers such as 453896.

## Comparison of length

- Tell the children to draw round their shoe and cut it out. Talk about burglars who leave clues behind; for example, footprints. Use the cutouts to compare, for example, two feet: Which is the longer? How could you test to see if you are correct? Check with a line of small objects. Repeat this activity using hands.

## Sequencing colours

- Talk about the colours in traffic lights. Using coloured beads or a pegboard, reproduce the pattern of traffic lights colours – start with red at the top, followed by amber, then green. Ask the children to repeat the pattern.

### Knowledge and Understanding of the World

*Find out about everyday technology.*

## Identity parade games

- You will need group photographs of the children standing in a line (suggest eight children). Talk about how we are all different. Introduce the idea of identity parades and witnesses.

### Game 1

- Select one of the group photographs and send those children out of the room with an adult. The rest of the class sit facing the door. Tell one of the group waiting outside the classroom to peep around the door, giving the rest of the class just a quick glimpse. The children then turn round and identify that child on the photograph.

### Game 2

- Select one of the group photographs and fix it to a board in front of the class. The teacher briefly holds up one of the individual photographs. The children

**Starting** with role play – Emergency 999

# Making posters and ID cards

have to identify that child from the group photograph.

**Fingerprints**

❏ Discuss how the police solve crimes. They look for clues at the scene of the crime, such as fingerprints, footprints or items left behind. If possible, show pictures of fingerprints and footprints. Explain how when we touch things we leave a mark, our fingerprint. Talk about how the police dust for fingerprints.

**Footprints**

❏ Make a small collection of shoes with patterned soles. Prepare a tray containing talcum powder. Ask the children to press each shoe into the tray and print it on black sugar paper. Display these prints in the police station. (Fix the prints with hairspray.) Ask the children to look closely at the patterns on the soles and to match them with the prints.

**ICT**

❏ Visit the Cbeebies website (see Resources) and play detective games with PC Plum: 'The Stolen Cushion', 'The Missing Red Ball' and 'The Lost Hamster'.

## Communication, Language and Literacy

*Speak clearly and audibly with confidence and control and show awareness of the listener.*

**Listening game**

❏ Provide a screen in the police station; for example, a large piece of fabric draped over the desk. Sit three children behind the screen and a group of children in front, as police. Ask the children behind the screen, one at a time, to describe themselves. For example, 'I have blond hair and blue eyes.' (There is no need to give too many clues as the object of the game is to listen carefully to the voice.) Ask, 'Who can guess who was speaking?' Extend this activity by asking the children to try and disguise their voice. They might whisper, raise or lower their voice, or talk through their hand. Develop this further by recording individual children story telling, singing or reading. Play back the recordings at random. Ask: Who do you think that was? How do you know?

**Talking**

❏ Using either a set of commercial photographs of faces or pictures from a magazine, help the children to provide accurate descriptions; for example, long hair, white skin and blue eyes.

**Supported writing: creating ID cards**

❏ Talk to the children about the purpose of identity cards. Using the card on page 36 and either small photos of the children or faces cut out from magazines, demonstrate how to complete an identity card, adding the cardholder's details. Store the identity cards in an open-topped cardboard box in the police station and encourage children to flick through the cards, looking for a particular person.

**Completing a work schedule**

❏ Place a whiteboard in the police station. Divide the board down the middle with coloured tape; label one side 'day' and the other 'night'. Talk about how most police stations have to be open at all times and how police officers work in shifts. Encourage the children to use the board, organising their shifts. They can write names on the whiteboard, referring to the ID cards if they wish.

**Emergent writing**

❏ Provide either bought or homemade pads of paper for 'police notebooks' and a variety of pens and pencils. Encourage the children to use these when acting as a police officer to record incidents.

# Making posters and ID cards

### Writing lists

❏ In the role play area, encourage the police officers to make lists of stolen property described by visiting 'members of the public'.

### Lost and found

❏ Make enough copies of the pictures of getaway cars on page 36 to have 24 cars. Colour pairs of cars identically but differently from the others. For example, one pair with striped markings, another pair with yellow wheels and so on. Glue one set of 12 cars onto A4 paper and slip them into a plastic wallet in a folder labelled 'cars'. Glue the other set onto small cards and laminate. The cards should be stored in a labelled box, just outside the police station. A child selects a card and takes it into the police station. He does not allow the police officer to see it. He tells the officer that he has lost his car. The child then describes the car on the card and the officer checks through the folder to see if it has been found. When he finds the car, they check to see if the pictures match.

### Physical Development

*Use a range of large apparatus. Travel around, under, over and through balancing and climbing equipment.*

### Movement

❏ Show the children how to carry mats and benches safely. Set out the apparatus to give opportunities to travel over, under and through. Add hoops, ropes, cones or markers. Suggest to the children that they are going to be police officers searching for a lost animal. They must move carefully in, out, over, under and through the apparatus, looking and searching, always being careful not to touch anybody as they go. On the command 'STOP' they must keep quite still.

**Extension**

❏ Try this activity in pairs, moving and searching together.

### Cutting skills

❏ Cutting out shoe templates (see Mathematical Development).

### Outside

❏ Say the chant: Red means stop. Green means go. Amber means wait. Even if you're late! Talk about hand signals, traffic lights and speed cameras. Some children can go on bikes or other ride-on vehicles, and 'police' in costume can try to direct the traffic. Tell the children that they must obey the police officer and follow his or her instructions. If you do not have a set of traffic lights, see page 32.

❏ Mark out parking bays with chalk. Make them quite narrow so the children are challenged when parking. Can they reverse into the parking bays?

**Starting** with role play – Emergency 999   15

# Emergency 999

## WEEK 3

**The role play area**

During this week the children will consider the work of the fire service, its role in society and the people who work in it. They will convert the police station into a fire station, with a firefighters' pole and a fire engine made from cardboard boxes. Use the splatter paint background of the police station but replace the police figures with figures of firefighters. Choose one of the buildings in the window of the role play area to be on fire. Ask the children to help you to make tissue paper flames in red and orange to stick around the building.

The children will make life-size firefighters, a **firefighters' pole** and **junk models** of fire engines. They will create a **fire engine with a ladder** from cardboard boxes or foam blocks and make a **collage picture**. Through role play they will have opportunities to explore fire-fighting, the emergency service and danger from fire.

### Resources

Photocopiable:

Poems and songs 2 (page 37)

Fiction books:

*The Life of St George*, Heinemann Library (0 431180 80 6)
*George and the Dragon* by Chris Wormell, Red Fox (0 099417 66 9)
*Fireman Fergus* by Mandy Ross, Ladybird (0 721421 65 2)

Non fiction books:

*People who help us: Fire Service*, Wayland (0 750222 53 0)
*Mapwork First Stages: In the town* and *In the country*, by Benedict Blathwayt, OUP (0 199106 71 1 and 0 199106 73 8)
*Firefighters* by Kate Daynes, Usborne Beginners (0 746061 27 7)
*Machines at Work: Fire Engine* by Caroline Bingham, Dorling Kindersley (0 751364 97 5)

**Websites:** www.preschooleducation.com and www.kinderkorner.com

Materials:

- Plastic tubing
- Wooden blocks
- Stopwatch
- Pictures of firefighters, fire engines
- Telephone
- Town mat
- Water pistols
- Fabric pieces and collage materials
- Dowelling poles
- Large cardboard boxes
- Red, yellow and orange tissue paper

Costumes and props:

- Firefighters' tabards and helmets
- Wellington boots
- Gloves
- Torches
- Whistles

# Creating a fire station

## Personal, Social and Emotional Development

*Initiate ideas and speak in a familiar group.*

### Circle time

- Consider and talk about the work of the fire service.
- Ask children if they think a firefighter's job is dangerous and if so, why. Can they think of other jobs that are dangerous? Talk about bravery: What does it mean to be brave? Do they know anyone who is or was brave? (Encourage them to think in general terms – perhaps a child who has just learned how to ride a bike without stabilisers and has practised hard even though he kept falling off.)
- If possible, read the story of St George (see Resources) Introduce the story of St George. Talk about St George as the patron saint of England and say that 23rd April is St George's Day when we celebrate his bravery, defeating the fiery dragon. (Link this with firefighters putting out a fire.)

## Creative Development

*Explore colour, texture, shape, form and space in two and three dimensions.*

### Making junk model fire engines

- Paint a large box red. Show the children pictures of fire engines. Ask them to think of features they need to add. Can they select their own materials from a collection of boxes, tubes, hose pipe and so on? Ask them to make a ladder for the fire engine. Give lengths of cardboard tubing and masking tape. Encourage the children to play with the fire engine outside.

### Life-size pictures

- Show the children pictures of firefighters in uniform and discuss all the features of the uniform. As in Week 1, create life-size firefighters by drawing round a child. Paint the figures with black and yellow paint and add features such as breathing apparatus and helmets, and tools such as axes, using junk modelling and collage materials.

### Creating a firefighters' pole

- Place a long cardboard tube (perhaps from a fabric supplier) in the fire station as the firefighters' pole that enables them to get from the living quarters to the fire engine. This can be fixed to the wall or in a corner as children will not be expected to actually use it! The pole could be covered in tinfoil to give the effect of metal.

### Painting

- Paint pictures of a fire-breathing dragon.

### Collage

- Make collage pictures of fire-fighting. On paper, glue silhouettes of buildings drawn on and cut out of black paper. Add a fire engine (made from shiny red gummed paper or red felt). Add firefighters cut out from black paper and add features; for example, yellow helmets made from gummed paper and hoses from straws or pipe cleaners. Add flames with red, yellow and orange tissue paper.

**Starting** with role play – Emergency 999

# Creating a fire station

## Mathematical Development

*Use developing mathematical ideas and methods to solve practical problems.*

### Investigating length

- Have available a selection of lengths of plastic tubing, representing fire hoses. Ask the children to find the longest/shortest hose. This is more challenging if the tubing has been coiled. They could be asked to find a way of comparing the tubes. (Perhaps with a friend or taping ends to the table.)
- Tape various lengths of tubing to the edge of a table. Sticky tack wooden blocks or small buildings around the table. Give the children the opportunity and time to experiment and investigate – which hose pipes can reach each building? Ask them to describe their findings. Can any of the hoses reach all the buildings?

- Have available balls of wool or string. Challenge the children to cut lengths of wool; for example, longer than this book; shorter than this ruler. Tell them that a fire has started in an area of the classroom. How long should their hose be?

### Outside activity

- Have a starting point and a destination (for example, the 'fire engine' and a 'building' in the playground). Ask the children to guess how many paces the firefighter will have to take to get from the fire engine to the burning building. Estimate steps and strides. Will the firefighter get there quicker if he runs or walks? Let's try!

### Extension

- Let more able children use a stopwatch to check the estimates and record the times.

## Communication, Language and Literacy

*Enjoy listening to and using spoken and written language.*

### Listening

- Select one or two of the poems or songs from page 37. Encourage the children to learn one by heart.

### Vocabulary extension

- Look at a non-fiction book about fire-fighting (see Resources) and introduce vocabulary relating to fire: heat, flames, smoke, burning, danger and so on.

### Scribed writing

- Together make up a story about Firefighter Jo. Describing how one day Jo was cleaning the fire engine and checking all the equipment. He had just sat down to have a nice cup of tea when the emergency 999 call came through. Ask the children to say what happened next. Encourage them to consider the sequence of events and to use some of the vocabulary discussed earlier. Orally rehearse each sentence before you write it on the board and discuss aspects of writing such as capital letters, direction of print and so on.

### Sequencing

- Tell the children to make a series of pictures to tell the events of the story. Divide the story into sections; for example: 1. The telephone rang. Someone had called 999 and asked for the fire service. 2. Firefighter Jo put on his boots and helmet. 3. He slid down the pole, and so on. Let the children illustrate each section of the story and put them in the correct order. Display them around the room out of order and make a trail of wool for the children to indicate the sequence.

# Creating a fire station

## Independent writing

- Ask pairs of children to write a sentence to accompany their picture. Remind them of the scribed text created earlier and to use some of the vocabulary discussed earlier. Support some children by writing their text in highlighter pen and asking them to go over it in pencil.

### Extension

- Encourage the children to write sentences about St George and the dragon on strips of paper. These sentences can be used to annotate the pictures (see Creative Development).

## Knowledge and Understanding of the World

*Ask questions about why things happen and how things work.*

### Discussion

- Talk to the children about fire. What does it do? Who works in the fire service? Why do we need a fire service? How do firefighters help us (saving lives, saving property)? Talk about the fire station and the sequence of activities in a firefighter's day.

### Vocabulary extension

- Look at pictures of fire engines. Talk about the equipment and its purpose. Look at pictures of firefighters. Talk about their uniform and equipment. For example, ask why firefighters wear helmets and why the helmets are that particular shape and colour. Discuss how the firefighter puts out fires. Do they always use water? Talk about fire extinguishers in school. Talk about forest fires, fire services at airports and so on.

### Emergency calls

- Ask the children 'How do you call the fire brigade?', 'When should you call the fire brigade?' and 'What should you say to the operator in the call centre?'
- Demonstrate for the children how to use the play telephone to dial 999. Speak to an operator and give directions to get to the fire. The children who are 'firefighters' could pretend to climb down the pole, quickly dress in their firefighter's uniforms and set off in the fire engine to the fire.

### Using a town mat

- If you have a town mat encourage the children to help the firefighters find places. Give a starting and a finishing point and help them to use appropriate language, such as 'Go past the shops, over the railway and the fire is in a factory next to a church.'
- If possible, share either the 'In the town' or the 'In the country' Mapwork book (see Resources).

## Physical Development

*Move with confidence, imagination and in safety.*

### Dance

- Play music such as Stravinsky's 'The Firebird' or other suitable music. Encourage the children to pretend to be flames, starting small and getting bigger and bigger. Then they could pretend to be water splashing on the flames and putting them out.

### Outside

- Give a group of children water pistols. On a wall, draw buildings in chalk. Ask the children to aim the water pistols at the buildings. Can they wash off the chalk marks? Move further away. Is it easier or more difficult? Compare actions with your friends. Who is the most accurate?

### Racing games

- Say, 'Pretend you are firefighters, racing to the fire. Who will get there first?'

# Emergency 999

## WEEK 4

**The role play area**

The role play area will be used to reinforce learning through drama and imaginative play. The children take on the role of firefighters, responding to emergency calls, sliding down a pole and hurrying to the scene in a fire engine.

During this week the children will consider fire safety in the home and the environment. They will produce charcoal drawings of fire engines and firefighters, make **fire safety posters** and create **pictures** using many shades of orange, produced by mixing colours, to represent flames.

## Resources

Photocopiables:

Poems and songs 2 and 3 (pages 37 and 38)

Fiction books:

*The Forgetful Little Fireman* (book and tape) by Alan Macdonald, Ladybird (0 721419 26 7)
*Flashing Fire Engines* by Tony Mitton, Kingfisher (0 753402 98 X)
*Fireman Piggy Wiggy* by Ian Wybrow, Little Tiger Press (1 854306 98 7)

Non-fiction books:

*A day in the life of a firefighter* by Carol Watson, Franklin Watts (0 749636 18 1)
*Firefighters – People Who Help Us*, Franklin Watts (0 749646 69 1)
*Firefighter – Amazing Pop-Up Book*, Dorling Kindersley (0 751369 72 1)
*Big Machines: Fire Engines*, Franklin Watts (0 749655 64 X)

Audiovisual:

Any of the 'Fireman Sam' videos

Materials:

- Charcoal sticks for drawing
- Candle
- Roamer
- Posters about the danger of fire
- Smoke alarm
- Playground chalks
- Bucket
- Water pistols (empty washing-up liquid bottles)

*Starting with role play – Emergency 999*

# Safety in the home

## Creative Development

*Use their imagination in art.*

### Mixing colours

- Light a candle and ask the children to observe the colours in the flame. Model for them how to draw the candle and colour the flame. Explain that they will be making different shades of orange, using paints. Show the children a chart you have made, showing the different shades of orange. Ask them to mix red and yellow paint in different proportions. What happens if they add a little brown paint? Ask them to match the colours they make with your chart. Encourage them to fill a whole page, using different shades of orange. Display these in the role play area.

### Charcoal drawings

- Talk to the children about how burning wood turns it into ashes and charcoal. Let them experiment with making marks using charcoal. Tell them to use their fingers or a piece of kitchen paper to smudge the drawings. Ask them to draw pictures of buildings, fire engines and firefighters with charcoal. Try smudging the fire engine horizontally. Does it make it look as if it is moving? Display the pictures in the role play area or around the classroom.

## Personal, Social and Emotional Development

*Continue to be interested, excited and motivated to learn.*

### Circle time

- Discuss with the children the dangers of fire and playing with matches and lighters. Ask them why they think fires and heaters often have fireguards around them. Talk about the fire drill at school. If appropriate, have a practice of the procedures. Why do people have smoke alarms? What do they sound like? Talk about safety with bonfires and barbecues.

## Mathematical Development

*Say and use number names in order, in familiar contexts.*

### Counting

- Draw pictures of different sized ladders and helmets on thin yellow card. Laminate the pictures and cut them out. Demonstrate how to count the rungs by placing a helmet on the bottom rung and moving it up the ladder, counting as you go. Ask the children to do the same. Then ask them to put the helmet on the first or second rung and so on.

- Compare the lengths of the ladders. Which is the longest/shortest ladder? Can you put the ladders in order of length?
- How many Unifix bricks will you need if you put one on each rung of the ladder?
- Write the numbers on the rungs. (Use a dry wipe pen.)

### Extension

- Ask the children to count the number of rungs on one ladder and to write that number. Then ask them to count the number of rungs on a second ladder and to add that number to the first number. They should write this as a sum, such as 7 + 5= 12.

### Estimating height

- Build towers of different heights with small wooden blocks or Unifix. Which ladders will reach the top of each tower?

# Safety in the home

### Counting rhyme
- Select a counting rhyme from page 37 and read it with the children.

### ICT
- Program Roamer forwards and backwards from the fire station to the fire. (Perhaps put a small container of water, a ladder or a fireman's helmet on Roamer.)

## Communication, Language and Literacy

*Attempt writing for different purposes, using features of different forms.*

### Listening
- Read a story about a firefighter (see Resources).
- Listen to the taped version of *The Forgetful Little Fireman* (or similar). Discuss the story with the children and encourage them to retell the events in order.
- If possible, watch a 'Fireman Sam' video.
- Select a poem or song for children to learn, from pages 37 and 38.

### Drama
- Invite the children to re-enact one of the stories they have heard.

### Vocabulary extension
- Light a candle and look at the flame. Help the children to describe it. (Flickering, smoking, melting, burning and so on.)

### Demonstration writing: fire safety posters
- Show the children some simple posters and explain the purpose of a poster. Tell them they are going to help you to design a poster about safety near fire. You will need a large sheet of paper or a whiteboard. Draw a fire in the middle of the poster. Tell the children to turn to a partner and think of how to stay safe near fire. Share these ideas and write them around the picture of the fire – for example: 'Don't play with matches', 'Don't play near fires' and 'Don't play with candles'. Give each child a piece of paper and ask them to make their own posters. They should choose one of the rules and draw a picture to illustrate it. Display these posters in the fire station or around the room.

### Extension
- Make word cards based on the poster words, such as 'Don't play with matches'. Challenge the children to build sentences with the words. Turn over the key words ('Don't', 'play' and 'with') and ask the children to spell them from memory.

## Knowledge and Understanding of the World

*Ask questions about why things happen and how things work.*

### Dangers of fire
- Remind the children about how they discussed the dangers of fire. Talk about other causes of fires, such as electrical faults, and why we should not touch wires, plugs and sockets. Talk about the dangers in the kitchen, especially when cooking, and why we should not touch the cooker or pans on the hob. Reinforce not playing with matches.

### The Great Fire of London
- Tell the children the story of the Great Fire of London (1666) and explain how the buildings were too close together and made from wood. Try to find pictures of London around the time of the Great Fire. Tell them where the fire started (Pudding Lane) and how quickly it spread.

Starting *with role play – Emergency 999*

# Safety in the home

## Music and Song

- Sing the song 'London's Burning'. Sing it quietly at first and then loudly for 'Fire! Fire!'. Sing it as a round.

### Physical Development

*Move with control and coordination.*

## Fine motor control

- Charcoal drawings (See Creative Development).

## Play the firefighters game

- Talk about the actions of firefighters: holding the hose, crawling, climbing a ladder, walking along a narrow wall, running to the scene and sliding down the pole. Ask the children for other suggestions. You call out the actions and the children follow the instructions. When told to 'FREEZE' the children should hold their action shape. (This can be adapted so that anyone who moves on 'Freeze' is out.)

## Outside activity

- Provide a bucket of water and empty washing-up liquid bottles or water pistols. Set out small hoops at increasing distances. Tell the children to try to squirt the water into the hoops.
- Draw ladders in chalk on the playground. Number each rung. Ask the children to run up the rungs as quickly as possible. Then give instructions; for example, 'Run up to rung 6,' and 'Run down to rung 2.'

**Starting** *with role play – Emergency 999* 23

# Emergency 999

## WEEK 5

**The role play area**

During this week the background to the role play area will remain the fire station but activities will be concentrated on the ambulance service. Many of the activities hopefully can take place outdoors. The children will make **stretchers**, an **ambulance** and design the **interior**.

If possible, try to arrange a visit by paramedics to the school.

*ambulance interior*

*stretcher*

### Resources

Photocopiables:

Paramedics poem (page 34)
Pictures of dangers in the home (page 39)

Fiction books:

*Fizz the Fire Engine* by David Wojtowycz, Orchard Books (1 843622 84 X)

Non-fiction books:

*Ambulance team – A Day in the Life of*, Franklin Watts (0 749636 35 1)
*Ambulance – People who help us*, Franklin Watts (0 749646 70 5)
*Stay safe at home*, 'Little Nippers' series, Heinemann Library (0 431172 70 6)
*Stay safe at school*, 'Little Nippers' series, Heinemann Library (0 431172 72 2)

Materials:

- Tubing
- Dowelling poles or broom handles
- Fabric for stretchers
- Pictures and posters of ambulances and crews
- Large cardboard box or polystyrene blocks
- Telephone (and mobile phone)
- Large sheets of card for ambulance doors
- Self-adhesive Velcro
- Collage materials, including foil
- Strong magnets
- Plastic trays
- Permanent markers

Costumes and props:

- Green uniforms or tabards
- Reflective strips for clothing
- Armbands with red cross
- Toy medical sets
- Disposable gloves
- Bandages
- Slings
- X-ray

# Creating an ambulance

### Personal, Social and Emotional Development

*Continue to be interested, excited and motivated to learn.*

### Circle time

- Go round the group asking children to share experiences about accidents. Has anyone been to hospital after an accident? How did they get to hospital?
- Ask the children if they have seen an ambulance. What colour is it? How do they know it is an ambulance? Why does it have a blue flashing light and a siren?
- Talk about the role of the ambulance service. Ask the children if they have ever seen inside an ambulance.
- Ask the children where the ambulance crew take people. (To A & E at the hospital.)

### Danger in the home

- Enlarge a copy of page 39. Divide the class into six groups. Give each group one of the pictures and ask them to talk about what is dangerous in it. Move around each group and talk about safety features. Then invite one or two children from each group to talk about their picture. Explain that if a very bad accident happens at home then an adult will dial 999 and call an ambulance.

### Creative Development

*Explore colour, texture, shape, form and space in two or three dimensions.*

### Making an ambulance

- You will need a large box and paints. Turn the box inside out and reglue it. Show the children pictures of ambulances. What colour are they? Talk about the significance of the red cross. Paint the box and add features such as wheels, bumpers, number plates and words. Talk about how the word 'Ambulance' on the front of the vehicle is written in mirror writing. Ask the children why this might be. Write it for the children and then give them a small mirror to check the word. Then write it on the front of the ambulance (ƎƆИAJUᗺMA).

### Designing the inside of an ambulance

- Following discussion about the equipment needed in an ambulance, design and make an interactive picture. Draw the background of the inside of an ambulance (see illustration). Cut out large door shapes to cover the background. Staple the doors to the sides of the background so that they hinge. Draw on card the equipment for the ambulance – bed, pillow, stretcher, blanket, oxygen cylinder, seats, medical equipment, blood pressure monitor and drawers labelled 'bandages', 'needles', 'gloves' and 'medical supplies'. Cut this card out and laminate it. Fix hook Velcro pieces to the back of the equipment and loop Velcro pieces to the inside of the ambulance. Display the inside of the ambulance just above floor level so that the children can use it in their role play.

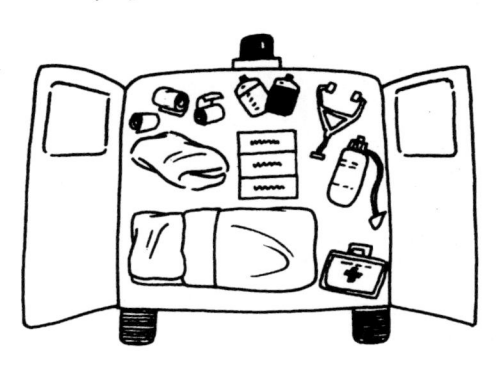

### Making a stretcher

- Make stretchers by stapling lengths of fabric to two dowelling poles or broom handles. Alternatively, make a stretcher using a coat and two poles.

### Magnetic game

- Give the children small pieces of paper and ask them to draw an ambulance and cut it out. Laminate them and fix a paperclip to the back. Draw simple roads on the plastic trays, such as from the ambulance station to the scene of an accident. Use permanent markers for this. Challenge the children to use a magnet under the tray to take an ambulance along the roads to the accident.

Starting with role play – Emergency 999   25

# Creating an ambulance

## Mathematical Development

*Use developing mathematical ideas and methods to solve practical problems.*

### Roamer

- Tape a red cross and a small box onto Roamer. Place a small bandage inside the box. Show the children how to program Roamer to move forwards and backwards. Estimate distances from, for example, the ambulance station to a child. Program Roamer and test the estimates. Can they send Roamer back to the ambulance station?

### Length

- Roll fairly short lengths of bandage and ask the children to estimate which is the longest and which is the shortest. Ask them how they can test their estimates. How will they measure the bandages? Can they put the bandages in order of length?

### Splints

- Have available a selection of items that could act as splints for a doll; for example, lolly sticks, matchsticks, pieces of thin dowelling and pencils. Ask the children which is the longest and which the shortest. Can they display them in length order?

#### Extension

- Number each set of splints and support the children as they record the differences in length between the different splints. Discuss how this information can be displayed, such as in a graph or table.
- Say and act out the paramedics poem from page 34.

## Communication, Language and Literacy

*Use language to imagine and recreate roles and experiences.*

### Speaking and listening

- Using the telephones in the role play area, help the children to dial 999. Role play with them either as the operator or as the caller. When they are confident at making and responding to calls, record some of the conversations. Let them play back these conversations in their imaginative play.

### Reading for meaning

- Write a brief account of an ambulance officer's day leaving spaces for high frequency words. For example:

    'I __ (am) a paramedic. We got __ (a) 999 call. We ___ (went) in the ambulance. The man ___ (had) a broken leg. We put ___ (the) man on a stretcher. We turned ___ (on) the siren. We rushed __ (to) the hospital.'

    Make separate word cards for the high frequency words. Give out the cards to pairs of children. As you read the account, ask them to discuss whether their word fits the gap. Ask them to come out and fix their word in the gap and read the sentence together.

#### Extension

- Ask the children to write the missing words on a whiteboard.

### Writing labels

- Discuss with the children the names of all the items to go in the ambulance (see Creative Development). Demonstrate writing the labels for the equipment to go inside the ambulance. Talk about initial phonemes for each item. Laminate the labels and fix with sticky tack so that children can attach them to the appropriate objects inside the ambulance.

#### Extension

- Make a second set of labels and encourage the children to match the words.

Starting with role play – Emergency 999

# Creating an ambulance

## Knowledge and Understanding of the World

*Find out about and identify objects and events they observe.*

### Listening

- Share a non-fiction book about ambulances and the ambulance service (see Resources).
- Show the children pictures of ambulances. Talk about emergencies and the emergency services.
- Talk about accidents on the road, in the home, at work and at school.

### Ambulances and ambulance crews

- Look at pictures of ambulance crews. Explain that some crews are called 'paramedics'. Look at their uniforms. Why do they wear uniforms?
- Brainstorm the equipment needed and carried in ambulances: blankets, stretchers, masks, gloves, bandages and so on. Show the children as many examples of these as possible.

### Stretchers

- Ask the children how a patient is carried to the ambulance. Using one of the stretchers made in Creative Development, demonstrate how to carry a doll on a stretcher. Emphasise to the class that they must not try to carry another child, only dolls.

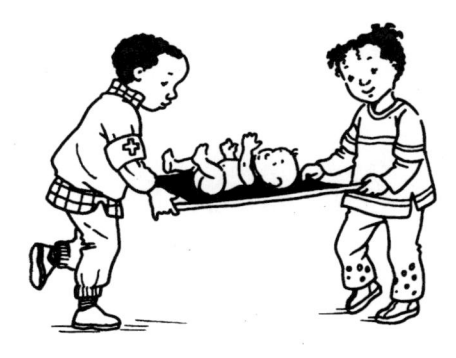

### Splints

- Talk about splints. Explain how they are used to stabilise a broken bone in an arm or a leg. If possible, show the class an X-ray.

### First aid

- Ask the children what they think 'first aid' means. Relate this to first aid in school. Talk about what happens if you fall over in the playground. Who looks after you? If you had a really bad accident at school, the first aider would call an ambulance and make sure that you were safe and as comfortable as possible until the ambulance arrived.

### Emergency

- Talk about emergencies. Can the children give examples? Tell them that ambulance crews have to be ready at all times in case they are called out.

## Physical Development

*Move with coordination and control.*

### Fine motor control

- Make dough models of an ambulance and the ambulance crew.
- Bandage a splint onto a doll, using short lengths of bandage, some lolly sticks and safety pins.
- Demonstrate how to make a sling, using triangular pieces of fabric and safety pins. Ask the children to make a sling for a friend.

### Construction kits

- Using building blocks, make ambulances, fire engines or police cars that move.

### Outside play

- Recreate a scene where a doll or a teddy is involved in an accident. Give some children roles as passers-by and others can be the ambulance crew. Take a phone into the playground so that someone can call the ambulance. Someone else could be an interviewer asking the crew what they are doing. If possible, have the sound effect of an ambulance to add authenticity. Encourage appropriate vocabulary, by asking questions such as 'How are you going to carry the person into the ambulance?'

# Emergency 999

## WEEK 6

**The role play area**

During this week the children will consolidate their learning about the three emergency services and also consider other people who help us. The role play area will display all the signs and objects that the children have made. The police station could be recreated to one side of the fire station. Display the blue lamp and notices in this area.

The children will undertake stretcher races. They will also write invitations and make **biscuits** and different **sandwiches** for a party to celebrate all the people who help us.

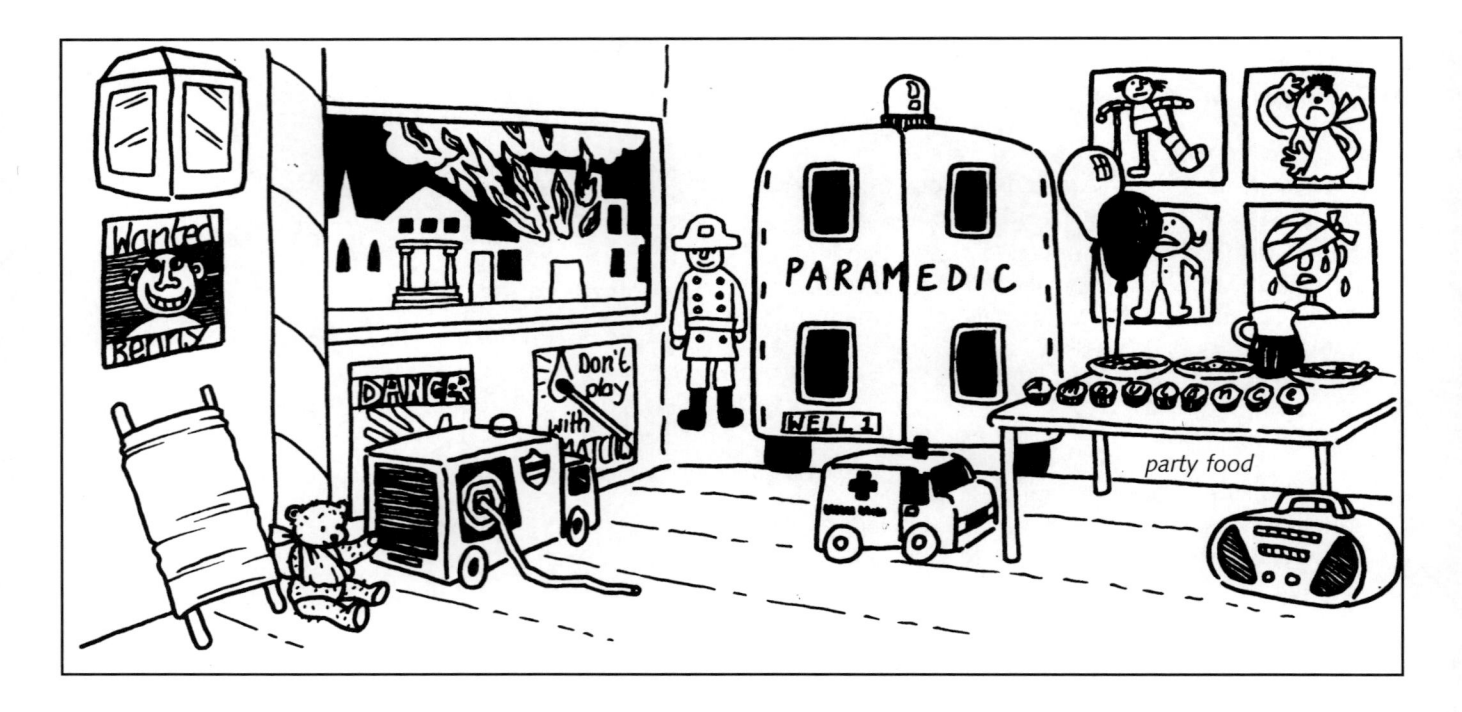

### Resources

Photocopiables:

Templates for invitations (page 40)
Emergency race game (page 41)
Traffic lights biscuits (page 42)

Books:

Display all the books used in this unit and encourage the children to browse through them. Reread some of the most popular stories, poems and information books.

Materials:

- Pictures and posters
- Tabards
- Small paperclips
- Fairy cakes and icing
- Bread, butter, cheese spread and jam
- 'Twiglets'
- Bandages
- Dolls
- Playground chalks
- Writing icing

28  Starting with role play – Emergency 999

# People who help us

## Personal, Social and Emotional Development

*Work as part of a group or class, taking turns and sharing fairly.*

### Circle time

- Remind the children about the many people who help us in our lives. Mime some actions and ask them to guess who it is; for example, a postal worker delivering letters, a refuse collector collecting bins and a vet caring for an animal. After the children have guessed one, let them join in with the mime. Write down the job titles of these people under the heading 'People who help us'. Add to the list throughout the week.

### Celebration party

- Tell the children that there is going to be a party at the end of the week to celebrate people who help us. They will decorate cakes and make food for the party. Ask them to think of a simple costume they could wear representing someone who helps us. Before the party talk about good table manners and general politeness to guests.

### Role hats

- Help the children to make simple hats from a band of cardboard with a cardboard sign indicating the role – teacher, vet, bus driver, train driver, hairdresser, crossing patrol warden. Put the hats in the middle of the circle and invite a child to choose a hat. Ask the child to sit on a chair in the middle of the circle while others ask questions about their job; for example, 'Where do you put the rubbish?', 'Do you like teaching?' and so on. Let as many children as are willing have a go in the role hot seat.

## Mathematical Development

*Recognise numerals 1–9.*

### Counting

- Emergency race game. Use the cards of vehicles on page 41 or use toy vehicles. Use the cards of men, women and burglars also on page 41. (Photocopy them onto card.) Cut out long strips of paper 8cm wide. Mark each strip of paper in 8cm squares. At one end put two matching vehicle cards (or toys) and at the other the appropriate person card. Tell the children to work in pairs. They choose their vehicle and take it in turns to throw a dice and move their vehicle the correct number of squares. The object is to be the first to reach the person.

### Sorting

- Put together a collection of different objects related to the 999 topic. Place these in the role play area. Put three hoops on the floor. Ask the children to sort the objects by which service they belong to.

**Extension**

- Remind the children about the list of people they suggested in Personal, Social and Emotional Development. Draw a simple block graph and write the job titles of the different people along the base of the graph. Ask the group to ask other children in their class which profession they would like to have when they grow up. Tell them to colour in a block for each child under the chosen job – police officer, nurse, vet, postal worker, firefighter, teacher, paramedic and so on.

# People who help us

## Communication, Language and Literacy

*Read a range of familiar and common words and simple sentences independently.*

### Sight words

- Using strips of card, demonstrate writing some simple sentences about the emergency services; for example, 'The firefighters put out fires,' and 'The paramedics help sick people.' Ask the children to suggest others and help them to shape their ideas into sentences. Cut up the sentences into separate words for them to rebuild and read.

**Extension**
- Challenge more able children to write some of the high frequency words from memory.

### Writing (Teacher modelling)

- Tell the children that they are going to write invitation cards. Draw a simple outline of a vehicle associated with one of the services on a whiteboard. Write 'You are invited to our party on ___ at ___ from ____ to _____'. Discuss how important it is to give the date, the place and the time in an invitation. Leave the completed invitation for the children to refer to when they make their own. Give each child a copy of one of the vehicles from page 40 to complete. Distribute them as appropriate.

### Listening

- Share with the children some of their favourite stories and poems read in the unit.

## Knowledge and Understanding of the World

*Find out about their environment and talk about features they like or dislike.*

### Role play

- Tell the children you are going to act out situations where the emergency services are required. They are to pretend to be operators answering 999 calls. You will dial 999 and say 'Hello, hello; please can someone help?' The children reply 'Which service do you require?' You then describe a situation – a cat is stuck in a tree or a man has been knocked off his bike or a robber has been seen running away from a house. The children respond, 'Then you need … (they select the appropriate service). Then they say, 'The … are on their way.'

### Helicopters

- Explain that not all rescue vehicles are road vehicles. Talk about police helicopters and air ambulances. They can cover long distances in a short time and can fly over the busy traffic. Look at pictures of helicopters and talk about rotor blades. Make a simple helicopter by taking a strip of paper 4cm wide. Cut into the strip to approximately 2/3rds down. Fold one flap forwards and the other backwards. Test your helicopter by holding it as high as you can and letting go. Observe what happens. Talk about your findings. Try attaching a small paperclip to the bottom of the strip. Test again and observe.

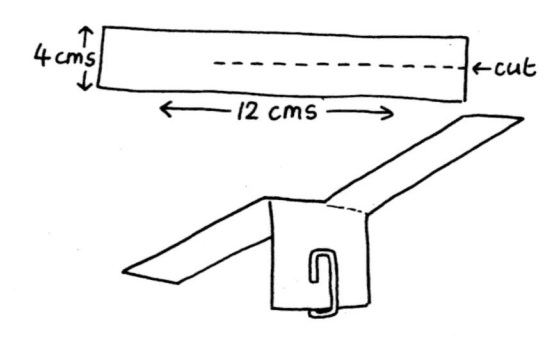

### Outdoor play

- Using playground chalks, designate areas in the playground as the police station, the fire station and the hospital. Encourage the children to move about on wheeled vehicles from one destination to another. Then give specific instructions; for example, 'You are an ambulance driver. Come from the hospital to the school and pick up a child with a broken leg. Take them back to the hospital.'

# People who help us

## Creative Development
*Use their imagination in art and design.*

### Party food
**(See Personal, Social and Emotional Development)**

- Give each child a ready-made fairy cake (available from most supermarkets). Have ready some white icing (just icing sugar and water) and tubes of writing icing. Display the words 'ambulance', 'police car' and 'fire engine'. Tell the children to cover the top of the cake with white icing. Allow this to dry. Then, using the writing icing ask children to write one letter per cake:
a m b u l a n c e
p o l i c e   c a r
f i r e   e n g i n e
Arrange the cakes on trays to spell out the words.

- Make 'bandage roll' sandwiches by spreading slices of bread with butter and jam. Cut off the crusts and roll. Press quite firmly and cut into small rolls. Place on trays, join side down.
- Provide 'Twiglets' as splints.
- Make 'sling' sandwiches by cutting white bread into triangles and spreading with cheese spread
- Make traffic lights biscuits (page 42). Read through the recipe with the children, telling them that this is a list of instructions. Tell them that they are going to make traffic lights biscuits together. Make the biscuits with small groups, following the instructions.

### Paintings

- Suggest the children complete paintings of incidents/accidents involving the emergency services.

### Outside play

- Encourage role play involving the three services outside in the garden or play area: provide a few props, such as tabards, the three model vehicles, a length of hose pipe and chairs.

## Physical Development
*Move with control and coordination.*

### Party games: 'Bandage the doll'

- You will need a doll, a roll of bandage, a laminated picture of an ambulance and some music. Sit the children in a circle. Place the roll of bandage and a doll in the middle. While the music plays, the children pass the ambulance around the circle. When the it stops, the child holding the ambulance starts wrapping the bandage around the doll. When the music starts again, he or she stops bandaging, rushes back to his or her place and continues passing the ambulance. The winner is the child who comes to the end of the bandage and holds the doll up!

### Party games: obstacle race

- 'Interservices' sports! Divide the children into teams: 'police', 'paramedics' and 'firefighters'. You will need costumes and props of equal numbers for each team. Lay the items at intervals in front of each team. The first child has to run and put on or pick up the first item, then run back to his team. The next child runs to pick up the next item of clothing or object and runs back to the start. Continue until each child has had a go and returned to his team.

### Party games: stretcher races

- Run some stretcher races. Use stretchers as made in Week 5. Put the children into pairs a distance away from, and opposite, a doll. Four pairs play the game at once. On the command 'GO' the children pick up their stretcher and race to pick up their doll.

Enjoy the party!

## Review and evaluation

*Encourage the children to reflect on the topic. What have they enjoyed learning about? Which part has been most exciting? Which stories and songs do they remember? Which artwork did they most enjoy doing? Which emergency services would they like to join?*

# The police station

### Instructions for creating the police station: the backdrop

- Line the walls of the police station with pale blue frieze or backing paper.
- Make the window. You will need: a large sheet of dark blue paper and another sheet of white paper the same size; old toothbrushes; rulers and some slightly watered down yellow ready-mix paint.
- Draw a skyline of buildings on the white paper and cut it out. Place the skyline on the blue paper and anchor at each corner. Dip a toothbrush into the paint. Drag a ruler towards yourself over the brush to splatter the paint. Continue splattering paint around the cutout, making the speckles most dense along the skyline. Allow the paint to dry. Remove the paper cutout. Windows etc can then be added, using shades of yellow paint, pastels, wax crayons or coloured pencils. You can add shading, lines to give definition to the buildings and smudged blocks of colour for windows. Vehicles could be added; dark shadowy shapes with headlights; a watery moon; a tree or streetlights.
- More able children could attempt a watery reflection using pastels.

### Making a blue light

- Make a blue light to hang outside the police station. Look at pictures of 'blue lights'. Find a box as near to the shape as possible. Turn the box inside out and reglue. Cut out holes for the glass on each side. Ask a child to paint the outside with blue paint. Ask others to find a way to measure the holes and cut pieces of blue cellophane to glue inside for the glass. Support as necessary. Fix a handle to the top and suspend above the entrance to the police station.

### Making traffic lights

- Paint circles of red, amber and green on a rectangle of black card and laminate. Using strong glue, a glue gun and/or a staple gun, fix the traffic lights to a dowelling pole. Laminate three sheets of black card and tape to make a hinged cover over the 'lights'. If possible push the pole into the ground for ease of use. If the covers do not stay closed, use sticky tack to hold them in place.

### Making a speed camera

- Make a speed camera with a box, painted yellow and place it in the outdoor area. Again, this could be fixed to a pole and set in the ground.

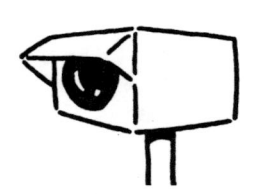

**Starting** *with role play*

Photocopiable

# Police officers

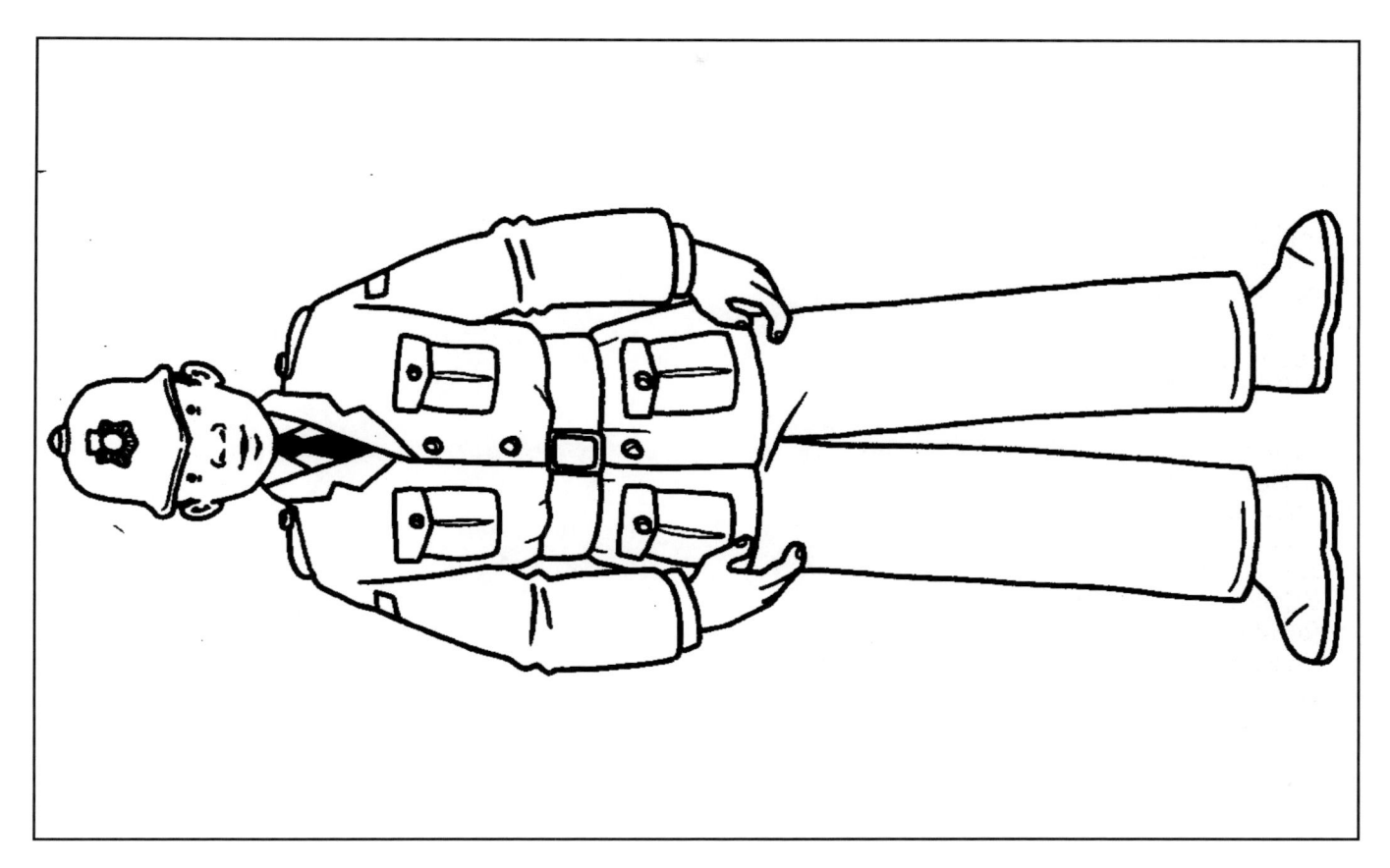

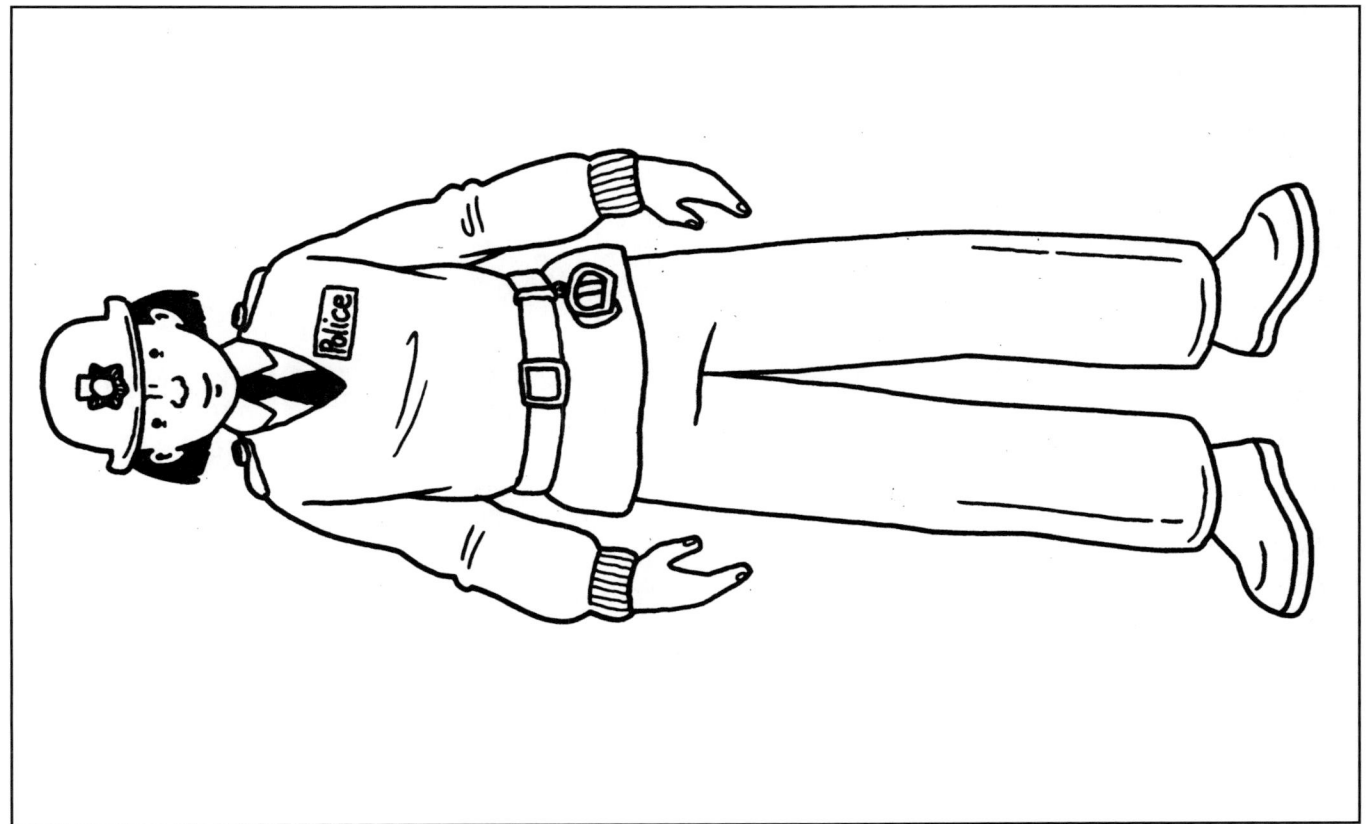

Starting *with role play*

# Poems and songs 1

### Ten tall policemen

Ten tall policemen were standing in a row
Two forgot their helmets
So they had to go.

Eight tall policemen were standing in a row
Two caught a cold
So they had to go.

Six tall policemen were standing in a row
Two saw a traffic jam
So they had to go.

Four tall policemen were standing in a row
Two had sore feet
So they had to go.

Two tall policemen were standing in a row
Both of them were hungry
So they had to go.

No tall policemen were standing in a row
They're back in the police station
That's where we'll have to go.

Maggie Hutchings

### I'm a tall policeman
(sung to the tune of 'I'm a little teapot')

I'm a tall policeman in my car.
I help people near and far.
If you have a problem, call on me.
And I will be there, 1, 2, 3!

I'm a policewoman dressed in blue.
If you're lost, I'll help you.
If you have a problem, call on me.
And I will be there, 1, 2, 3!

Maggie Hutchings

### The policeman

The policeman has many jobs.
They never seem to end.
But this you must remember:
The policeman is your friend.

Anon

### The neighbourhood policeman

There on the corner,
in his suit of blue,
The neighbourhood policeman
is there to help you.
If you get lost
he knows what to do.
Just tell him your name
and your address too!

(anon)

### Ten paramedics
(a counting poem)

Ten paramedics standing in a row
Two held a stretcher, ready to go.
Eight paramedics standing in a row
Two held a blanket, ready to go.
Six paramedics standing in a row
Two held an oxygen tank, ready to go.
Four paramedics standing in a row
Two held some bandages, ready to go.
Two paramedics standing in a row
Turned on the siren, off they go!
Nee-nah, nee-nah, nee-nah.

Dee Reid

# Police equipment

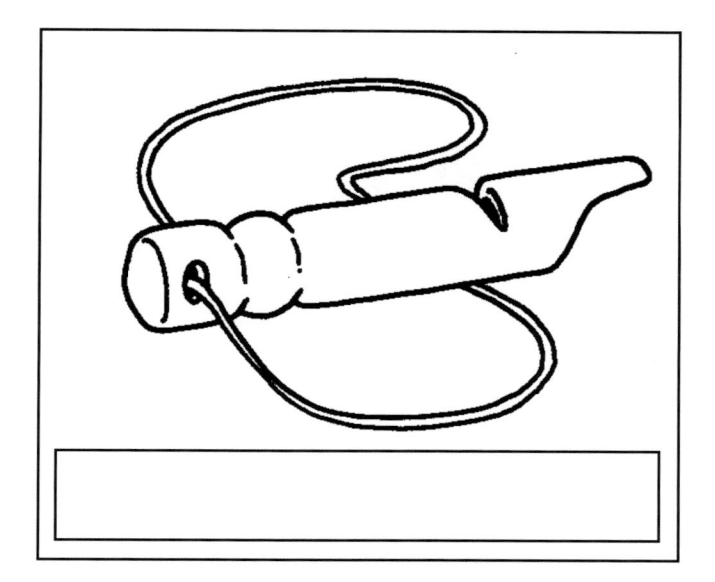

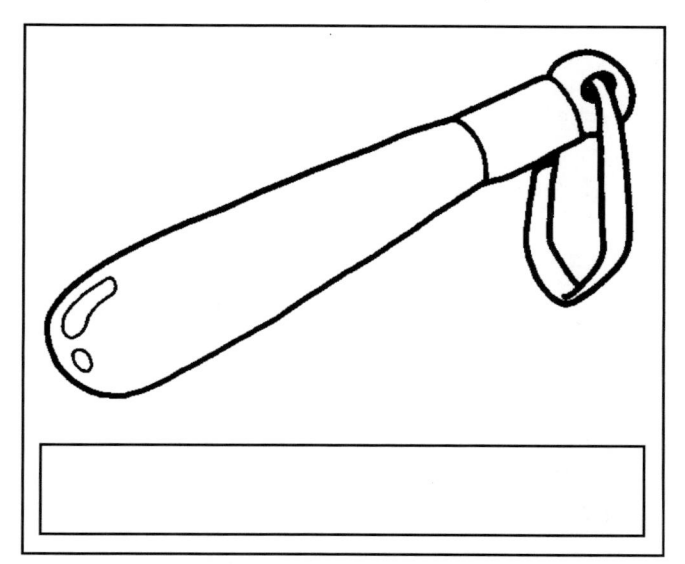

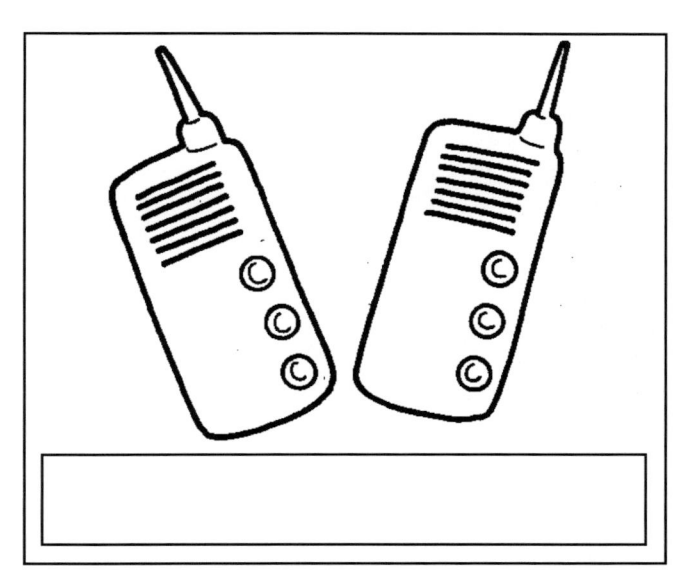

# Identity card and getaway cars

**IDENTITY CARD**

Name _____

Age _____

Height _____

Hair colour _____

Eye colour _____

Nationality _____

Address _____
_____
_____

Telephone number _____

photo

fingerprint

36  **Starting** *with role play*

Photocopiable

# Poems and songs 2

### I'm a little firefighter
(to the tune of 'I'm a little teapot')

I'm a little firefighter on the go
Here's my helmet, here's my hose
When I see a fire
Hear me SHOUT
I turn the water on
And put the fire out.
WOOSHSHSH

### I'm a firefighter
(to the tune of 'I'm a little teapot')

I'm a firefighter, my name is John
I put my boots and helmet on
I hurry to the fire and give a shout
Come on fire fighters put the fire out.

### Traditional rhyme (can be sung as a round)

London's burning, London's burning,
Fetch the engines, fetch the engines.
Fire! Fire! Fire! Fire!
Pour on water, pour on water.

### Five brave firefighters

Five brave firefighters
Tall and strong,
Climbed up the ladders,
Straight and long.
One found a fire
And put it out,
Water from his hose
Spurting out.
(four, three etc)

### Ten little firemen

Ten little firemen
Sleeping in a row.
Ding-dong goes the bell
And down the pole they go.
Off on the engine Oh! Oh! Oh!
Using the long hose so, so, so.
When the fire is out, home sooooo slow
Back to bed all in a row.

### Five little firefighters
(with hand actions)

Five little firefighters sitting very still
(hold up 5 fingers)
Until they see a fire on top of a hill.
Firefighter 1 rings the bell, ding, dong
(bend down thumb)
Firefighter 2 pulls his big boots on.
(bend down index finger)
Firefighter 3 says 'Don't delay.'
(bend down middle finger)
Firefighter 4 says 'I know the way.'
(bend down ring finger)
Firefighter 5 drives the truck to the fire
(bend down little finger)
The big yellow flames go higher and higher.
(spread arms)
Neeee-naw! Neeee-naw! Hear the fire truck say
As all the cars get out of the way.
Psssss! water from the fire hoses spouts
(rub hands together)
And quick as a wink the fire is out!
(clap hands)

### Firefighter, firefighter
(to the tune of 'Frére Jacques')

Firefighter, firefighter
You are so brave, you are so brave.
Putting out the fires
Helping all the people
Saving lives, saving lives.

# Poems and songs 3

**The Local Fire Brigade**

Help! Help! Help!

If your house has caught alight
In the middle of the night
Pick up a phone, call nine-nine-nine
We'll put it out in double quick time

*Cos we're the local fire brigade*
*We're quickly on the scene*
*We wear big hats and welly boots*
*And keep our hoses clean*

Help! Help! Help!

If your kitten's up a tree
Miaow, miaow, catastrophe
Pick up a phone, call nine-nine-nine
We'll rescue puss in double quick time

*Cos we're the local fire brigade*
*No emergency too small*
*We wear big hats and welly boots*
*And answer every call*

Help! Help! Help!

If little Jimmy's head is stuck
In the railings, you're in luck
Pick up a phone, call nine-nine-nine
We'll chop it off in double quick time

… Only joking

*Cos we're the local fire brigade*
*We answer every call*
*We wear big hats and welly boots*
*Except at the Firemen's Ball*

Help! Help! Help!

If your dog has gone astray
Not been seen since yesterday
Pick up a phone, call canine-nine-nine
We'll bring him home in double quick time

*Cos we're the local fire brigade*
*And when it's suppertime*
*Our mums and wives will let us know*
*By calling nine-nine-nine.*

Roger McGough

# Dangers in the home

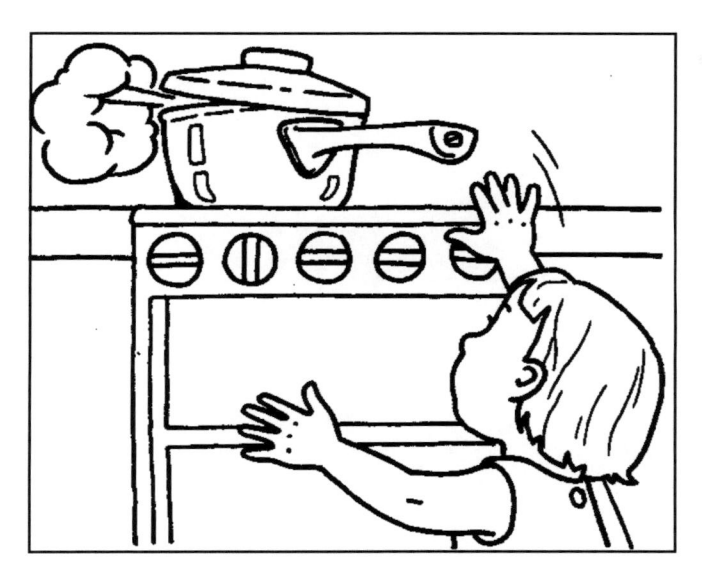

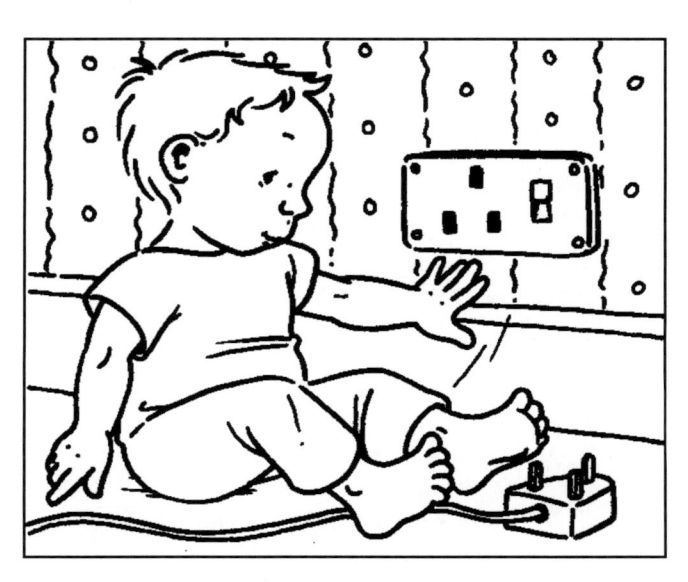

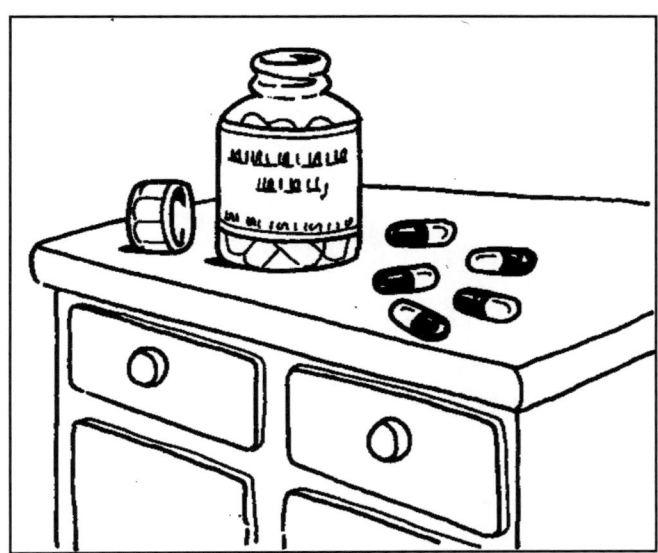

Starting with role play

# Invitations

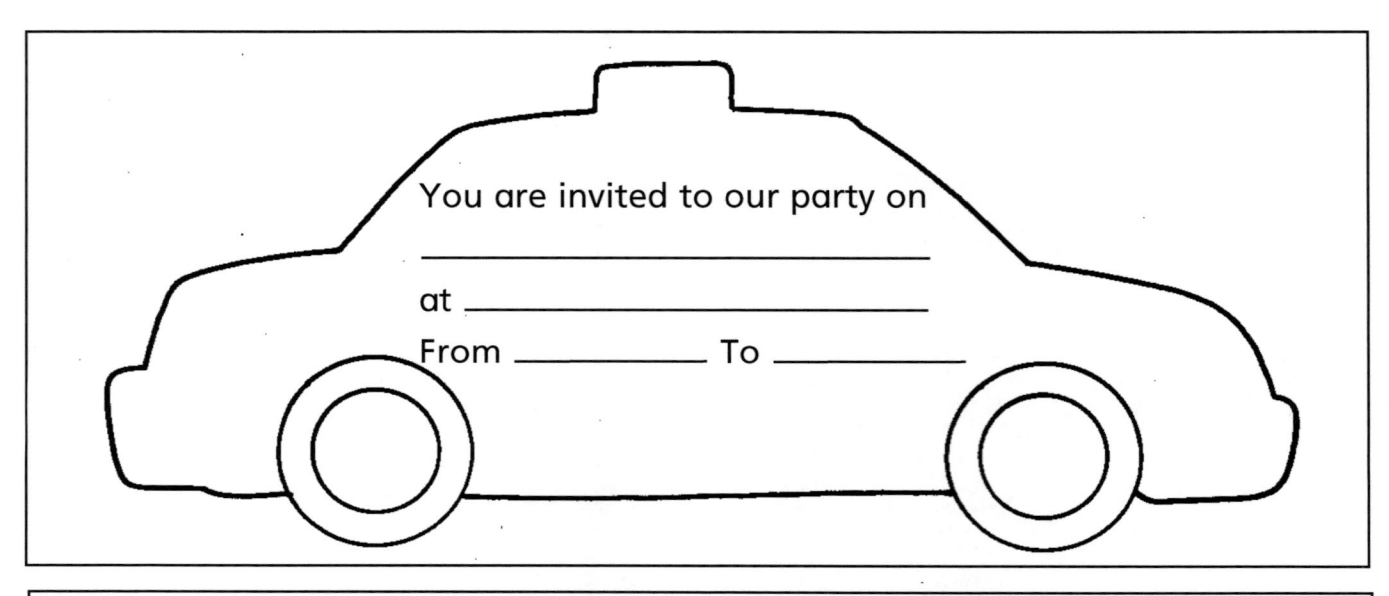

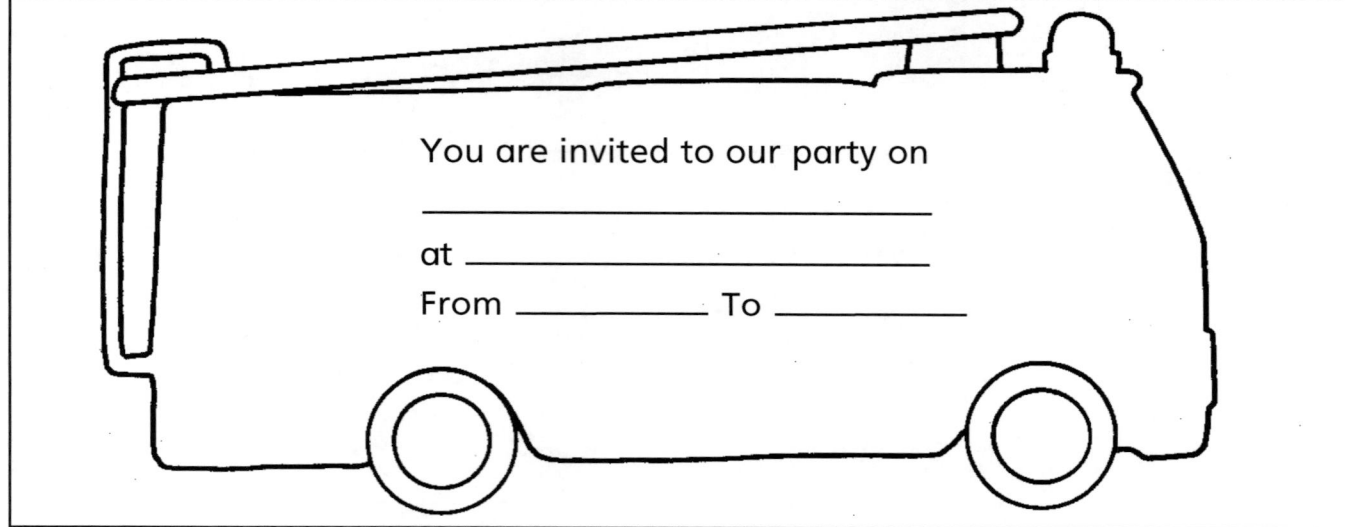

You are invited to our party on
_____
at _____
From _____ To _____

You are invited to our party on
_____
at _____
From _____ To _____

You are invited to our party on
_____
at _____
From _____ To _____

# Emergency race game

Starting with role play

# Biscuits

## Traffic lights biscuits

**What you need**
125g softened butter
50g caster sugar
175g plain flour
About a tablespoon of milk
Raspberry, apricot and greengage jams (or lime marmalade)

**What to do**
- Set the oven to 350°F/180°C/Gas Mark 4.
- Sieve flour into a mixing bowl.
- Stir in sugar.
- Cut up the butter.
- Rub the flour, sugar and butter together with the tips of your fingers until the mixture is like breadcrumbs.
- Add milk and mix everything together with your hands to make a ball of dough. (You may need to add a little more milk.)

- Cut the dough into two equal halves.
- Using a rectangular cutter, cut shapes out of one half of the dough.
- Using a small circular cutter, cut three vertical circles out of each rectangle of dough. (These circles are not needed for the traffic lights biscuits.)

- Using the same rectangular cutter, cut out from the other half of the dough the same number of rectangles.

- Place the shapes on a baking tray, lined with non-stick baking parchment.
- Bake in the oven for about 15 to 20 minutes, or until they are a pale golden colour.

- When the biscuits are cold, spread jam in traffic lights sequence over the plain rectangles, ie red, orange, green. Place 'holed' biscuits on top.

# One cut book

You will need:

❏ a piece of A3 paper

❏ scissors

What to do:

❏ Fold the paper in half lengthways, then in half widthways, then in half again widthways to form eight rectangles. (Figure 1)

*Figure 1*

❏ Open the paper and fold widthways, making a sharp crease. (Figure 2)

*Figure 2* fold → crease marks

❏ Cut from the folded edge to the 'cross' of the creases. (Figure 3)

*Figure 3* fold → cut to cross

❏ Open the paper completely and fold lengthways. Push left and right ends into the centre. (Figure 4)

*Figure 4* cut fold → push →

❏ Fold round to form front and back of book. (Figure 5)

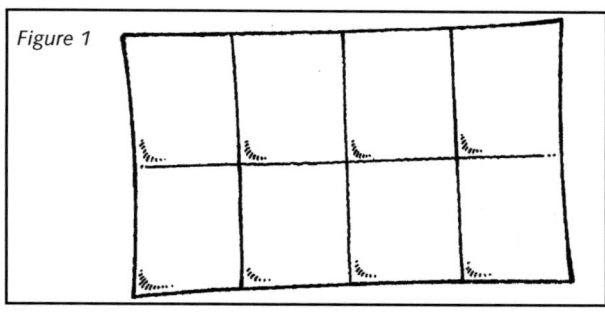

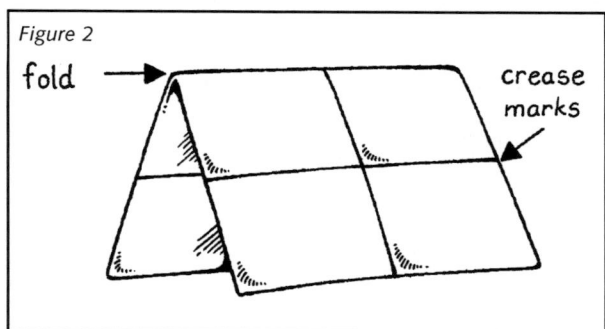

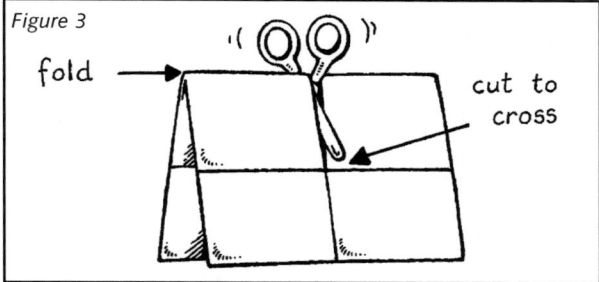

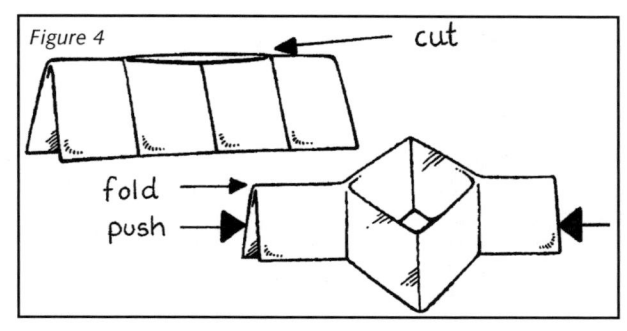

*Figure 5* crease firmly

**Starting** with role play

Unit: _____

# Observational Assessment Chart

Class: _____   Date: _____

| Name | Personal, Social and Emotional Development | Communication, Language and Literacy | Knowledge & Under-standing of the World | Mathematical Development | Creative Development | Physical Development |
|---|---|---|---|---|---|---|
| | Y B G ELG | Y B G ELG | Y B G ELG | Y B G ELG | Y B G ELG | Y B G ELG |
| | Y B G ELG | Y B G ELG | Y B G ELG | Y B G ELG | Y B G ELG | Y B G ELG |
| | Y B G ELG | Y B G ELG | Y B G ELG | Y B G ELG | Y B G ELG | Y B G ELG |
| | Y B G ELG | Y B G ELG | Y B G ELG | Y B G ELG | Y B G ELG | Y B G ELG |
| | Y B G ELG | Y B G ELG | Y B G ELG | Y B G ELG | Y B G ELG | Y B G ELG |
| | Y B G ELG | Y B G ELG | Y B G ELG | Y B G ELG | Y B G ELG | Y B G ELG |
| | Y B G ELG | Y B G ELG | Y B G ELG | Y B G ELG | Y B G ELG | Y B G ELG |
| | Y B G ELG | Y B G ELG | Y B G ELG | Y B G ELG | Y B G ELG | Y B G ELG |
| | Y B G ELG | Y B G ELG | Y B G ELG | Y B G ELG | Y B G ELG | Y B G ELG |
| | Y B G ELG | Y B G ELG | Y B G ELG | Y B G ELG | Y B G ELG | Y B G ELG |
| | Y B G ELG | Y B G ELG | Y B G ELG | Y B G ELG | Y B G ELG | Y B G ELG |
| | Y B G ELG | Y B G ELG | Y B G ELG | Y B G ELG | Y B G ELG | Y B G ELG |
| | Y B G ELG | Y B G ELG | Y B G ELG | Y B G ELG | Y B G ELG | Y B G ELG |

Circle the relevant Stepping Stones (Y = Yellow; B = Blue; G = Green or ELG = Early Learning Goal) and write a positive comment as evidence of achievement.